ONE-MINUTE
COUNSELOR™
for Men

H. NORMAN WRIGHT

HARVEST HOUSE PUBLISHERS
EUGENE, OREGON

Cover by Dugan Design Group, Bloomington, Minnesota

THE ONE-MINUTE COUNSELOR FOR MEN
Copyright © 2015 by H. Norman Wright
Published by Harvest House Publishers
Eugene, Oregon 97402
www.harvesthousepublishers.com

ISBN 978-0-7369-6106-6 (pbk.)
ISBN 978-0-7369-6107-3 (eBook)

Printed in the United States of America

15 16 17 18 19 20 21 22 23 / BP-JH / 10 9 8 7 6 5 4 3 2 1

Aging

"I'm getting old…older, and I don't like it. Each year it feels like I'm accomplishing less. Any suggestions?"

First, read Joshua 14:6-14. Did you notice Caleb's age? Did you notice the word "wholehearted" in relation to how he lived? Are you living wholeheartedly? This is the attitude God wants us to have about Him, about life, and about what we do—whether we're twenty or ninety. "Wholehearted" means being devoted, determined, enthusiastic, free from reserve and hesitation.

Here's the thing: We'll live differently, but *we won't live less.* Let's not overlook what we *can* do. Let's not fail to ask God to direct and guide our future. And there will be one!

> "I know the plans I have for you," declares the LORD, "plans to prosper you and not to harm you, plans to give you hope and a future" (Jeremiah 29:11).

There are minuses that arrive as we age, yet certainly there are pluses as well:

> You don't get old from living a particular number of years; you get old because you have deserted

your ideals. Years wrinkle your skin; renouncing your ideals wrinkles your soul. Worry, doubt, fear and despair are the enemies which slowly bring us down to the ground and turn us to dust before we die.[1]

We can approach growing older in several ways. One is grasping the past and holding on—refusing to relinquish being the main influence in family and social arenas, clinging to a job, denying limitations, or constantly informing others about accomplishments.

Another response is withdrawing into apathy and indifference. Usually the frozenness moves into regret, depression, and even bitterness.

A third approach (the healthiest one) is choosing life whatever that entails. This is being present—being active—in life. Ambition is still there, but now it's been redirected into new channels. There is discovery of new purposes and setting of new goals. There is *meaning* based on the furthering of God's kingdom.

Make the decision to live fully now even as you anticipate spending joyous eternity with Jesus Christ.

Anger

"I need help with anger. How do I keep it in check?"

Some people believe Christians should never get angry. But that's unrealistic and *not* something God expects from us. Anger isn't sinful; it's how we handle it that makes the difference.

Anger must be controlled so it doesn't become heated or unrestrained. Righteous anger motivates us to positive, unselfish action. Hatred, malice, and resentment aren't part of healthy anger. They contribute to strokes, heart attacks, high blood pressure, hypertension, colitis, and ulcers.

Scripture offers plenty of healthy guidelines for anger, including these verses from the book of Proverbs:

- An angry person stirs up conflict, and a hot-tempered person commits many sins (29:22).

- Do not make friends with a hot-tempered person, do not associate with one easily angered, or you may learn their ways...(22:24-25).

In *The Man in the Mirror*, Patrick Morley describes a scenario familiar to many men:

> Anger resides behind the closed doors of most

of our homes. Personally, I have never lost my temper at the office. I would never want my colleagues to think I couldn't control myself. But rarely a week goes by in which the sparks of family life don't provide good tinder for a roaring fire of anger...

Angry words are like irretrievable arrows released from an archer's bow. Once released, traveling through the air toward their target, they cannot be withdrawn, their damage cannot be undone. Like the arrows of the archer, our angry words pierce like a jagged blade, ripping at the heart of their target.

When anger pierces the soul of the home, the lifeblood of the family starts to drain away. You may notice that a secretary seems to find you attractive. You reflect on how your wife no longer appreciates you. It never occurs to you that it may be you, that if that secretary knew the real you—the angry you that lives secretly behind the closed doors of your home—she would find you about as desirable as a flat tire.[2]

That's sobering, isn't it?

Arguing

"Argue, argue, argue! That's the best way to describe our marriage. I used to believe it would change, but no such luck. It's like we both expect any interaction to end up chipping away at one another. I'm not sure she or I can change."

If you think nothing can change or improve your relationship, you're not alone. At one time or another most couples think that. But don't believe it! If you do, it may become a self-fulfilling prophecy. If you or anyone else believes that nothing can improve your marriage, test that belief! Challenge it! Argue with it! Commit *yourself* to change regardless of what your wife says or does.

Here are some ideas from several individuals who wanted to have discussions with their wives without getting into defensive arguments that seemed to erupt constantly (sound familiar?).

1. One husband worked on his self-talk. He made the decision to believe that his wife wasn't out to get him or simply to argue with him. He chose to believe she'd have good ideas. (When's the last time you let your wife know she had a helpful suggestion?)

2. Another husband committed himself *not* to: 1) interrupt; 2) argue or debate; 3) walk out. He

chose to listen. "To answer before listening—that is folly and shame" (Proverbs 18:13).

3. Another husband suggested that it works best to give feedback instead of remaining silent. During conversations he made comments like "that's interesting," "tell me more," and "I need a few minutes to think about that, but I will get back to you."

4. Another husband decided, "Even if this doesn't work the first time, I'll try it at least five times."

5. Another husband made the decision to thank his wife for her response in a discussion, even when her response was just minimal. I'm being more positive, he said.

What about you? What would you like to change in your conversations? Begin with identifying any basic beliefs that are negative. What can you do to change your pattern of discussions? Keep in mind that by modeling positive changes, you may influence your wife to follow your lead.

Cheating

"I know three friends who are cheating on their wives. One told me that I've probably cheated on my wife because there's more than one way to cheat. Is that true?"

You may never have cheated on your wife by being with another woman, but maybe you have in other ways. One man said, "I've been a workaholic. I haven't tended to my wife's needs. I haven't cared for her the way she needed me to. I've cheated on my wife—and I've cheated myself."

If we're that honest, perhaps we're a lot like this husband. We've all cheated our spouses in some form. You may not be physically cheating through adultery or pornography, but you may be cheating your marriage out of the God-honoring, God-designed life that it was meant to be. And that affects everything, even your sex life.

We cheat when we withhold affection and when we give too much of our time and energy to our kids or to others. We cheat when we connect emotionally with opposite-sex friends and colleagues. We cheat when we don't fully give ourselves sexually to our spouses. We cheat when we become selfish with our sexuality—when sex or the lack of sex becomes more about "me, me" than "we, we."

Cheating is serious business to God. When we cheat, we don't simply hurt our spouses. We also hurt our marriages, our relationship with God, and ourselves.

It's easy to blame someone or something other than ourselves when our sex lives aren't all we know they could be. We need to answer these questions honestly:

- How are we cheating ourselves out of a successful and satisfying sex life?

- How are we cheating ourselves individually?

- How are we cheating ourselves relationally, physically, and spiritually?

Is it by fantasizing? Is it withholding part of our hearts out of fear of becoming too vulnerable or getting hurt? Is it because of a spiritual gap that we've never filled? Is it that we're not fully present when we make love to our spouses because we're thinking about other things?

Redefining our definition of "cheat" means we admit, "My selfishness is cheating my spouse and me out of a great marriage and a great sex life. My selfishness is cheating me out of developing the character qualities that God wants me to have."[3] It's something to think about.

Cherishing

"How can I be sure I'm meeting my wife's needs? Most of my tries miss the bull's eye and some miss the target!"

Most of us need help with this area. To get rid of misunderstandings and faulty mind reading, it's far better to share with each other your needs, wants, and desires in a specific but non-demanding manner. When you search out your partner's wishes to meet them as best you can, you're implementing servanthood as portrayed in Scripture.

One of the most effective ways of meeting each other's love needs and wants is to launch into the "Cherishing Days" exercise. Sound interesting? It can be! And it's easy to implement. Each partner makes a list of fifteen small, positive behaviors he or she would enjoy receiving. These behaviors should have four characteristics:

1. They must be specific and positive. For example, a wife would like her husband to sit next to her on the couch as they watch the news after dinner. She's made a positive request for a desired behavior instead of complaining, "You ignore me and are preoccupied with TV."

2. The small, cherishing behaviors must not be concerned with past conflicts or old demands.

3. The positive behaviors must be such that they can be accomplished on an everyday basis.

4. The behaviors must be easily achievable—they don't require excessive time or expense.

Take several days to compile your lists. Think back to the most satisfying times of your courtship and marriage to discover ideas. Some of the behaviors you think of may seem trivial, but add them anyway as long as they reflect your personal wants and needs.

Once your lists of cherishing behaviors are completed, exchange them. Read them and think about them. Then discuss them. Be sure to include *how* you would like each behavior performed.

Now declare the next week "Cherishing Days." Commit to putting your spouse's list into practice. Accomplish as many of her cherishing behaviors on the list as possible. Focus your attention and energies on what *you're doing* for your spouse, not on what she's doing or not doing for you.

When a "cherish behavior" is given and accepted, the act is being reinforced with a positive response, which further encourages the giver to continue giving. As each of you gives and receives, your love will grow stronger.

Connecting

"I get together with other guys, but it feels like there's a wall between us. Why can't I get closer and connect?"

We men tend to play it safe and erect walls between others and ourselves. There are several barriers or walls we typically hide behind, and each one is a variation of a "No Trespassing" sign.

The wall of competition. Two men meet for the first time and introduce themselves. What is each one thinking? "Am I a better man than he is? If so, by how much? If not, how much less a man am I?" This wall contains bricks labeled "job," "title," "money," and "status symbols."

The wall of women. Some men use the women in their lives as buffers. These women could include wives, girlfriends, mothers, and work assistants. These men are shy or lack social skills. The women are used as peacemakers, go-betweens, and mediators. Also, women tend to keep conversations going.

The wall of fear is another common barrier. None of us enjoys rejection, judgment, or criticism. Whether we admit it or not, we're sensitive to what others think of us.

Many men feel discomfort with man-to-man relationships. The fear of relating and sharing deep feelings covers many issues. They live with the fear of being emotionally close and yet experience isolation and loneliness when they aren't. They're also reluctant to share their successes or times of delight because they don't want to appear boastful, or, worse, incite competition.

If a man is given a choice of confidants with whom to share fears, concerns, and doubts, he is twice as likely to talk to a woman as to a man. That's because men fear that if they get too close to other men and share their feelings, they might be suspected of being gay. In the United States, men consider touching all right on the playing field or when celebrating something extraordinary but nowhere else. In other countries, men often show their friendships with other men with warm hugs, touches, and clapping one another on the shoulder or back.[4]

In Western countries, a man doesn't openly express affection with other men because he fears being considered unmanly. Even within close relationships, verbal expressions of affection don't come easily. When a man does something for a friend, the friend will offer a compliment through an insult or share with another person or group how he feels about his friend rather than expressing his appreciation directly.

What about you? What walls are in your life? How about tearing them down?

Emotions

"My wife wants me to show my feelings. Sometimes I don't have the words. Besides, men don't share that stuff."

Many men today honestly don't know how to express their emotions. They've been raised emotionally sheltered or inhibited in some way. They've lost the distinction between thinking and feeling or they find excuses to avoid the deeper levels of conversation.

Consider this: *There is no aphrodisiac in the world as strong and powerful as an ongoing, deep level of communication that connects one person to another.* Sexual intimacy and fulfillment come from *conversational intimacy.* There are no shortcuts or techniques that can substitute for honest expressions of inner feelings. This concept is so important I recommend you read this paragraph again!

Yes, intimacy requires time, and energy, and the willingness to be a risk-taker. I've heard scores of reasons for avoiding conversational intimacy. Most excuses can be summed up under fear and lack of desire. We need to make time and take time.

We need to stop viewing feelings as enemies and start seeing them as allies. Think about these benefits:

- Feelings motivate people. They challenge us to

do our best and assist us in some of our greatest accomplishments. Tapping into feelings is a tremendous energy source.

- Feelings create a healthy environment. Ignoring feelings depletes energy, whereas by expressing them the air is cleared and we move on in life. We don't get stuck with excess baggage from the past. Expressing feelings is one of the best ways of reducing stress…

- Feelings help us make the correct decisions. Those who are in close touch with their feelings are more prepared to make difficult decisions and take important actions than those who are not.

- Feelings help to heal both old and new wounds. If you're hurt, you don't have to stay hurt. Feelings help us forgive others and also complete unfinished business.

- Feelings give us life, since they are an endless source of fresh new energy. They bring beauty into our souls.[5]

How will you initiate intimate conversation this week?

Emotions and Risk

"I'm hesitant to share my feelings. It seems risky."

You're not alone. Here are some responses gleaned from a national survey of more than 700 men.

- "I'll tell you what would help me share more with my wife. For me to open up with her, there has to be no risk. I can be honest, but I don't want to be hassled. I don't want to be judged for what I share. And I want to share for as long as I want—and then have the freedom to quit when I need to."

- "My wife is an expert on what is a 'feeling' and what isn't 'a feeling.' I've tried to tell her what's going on inside of me and she tells me, 'But that's not a feeling.'…I feel like giving up if I'm never going to get it right."

- "Yeah, I shared my feelings. I opened up about work and my frustrations, and she claimed I just wanted sympathy and attention. I tried to show her some love and attention and she said, 'You must want sex. You've got some other motive in mind.' I try to be what she wants, and I get criti-cized because my motives are suspect."

- "It's important first to define the issues clearly. I

don't think women do this very well. They latch on to the first thing that comes to mind and get totally emotionally involved in it. The next thing you know, you're arguing about everything under the sun, and no one is happy."

- "She expects me to have all these reactions right at my fingertips and be able to call them up on the spot. Well, I can't do that. I don't operate the way she does. I need a little more time to think things through. I don't want to say something I'm going to regret later on. Somehow she has the idea that wanting time to think is not being open and honest."

Risk is a big factor in a man–woman relationship. Men are risk takers in many other areas of life, but only when we have resources we can fall back on. Many men feel that sharing feelings is like being on the brink of an abyss.

What can you do? Be honest. Let her know sharing feels risky, but you're willing to work on it. Tell her that it helps you when she listens and encourages you. Don't get sidetracked into arguments. Instead, gently repeat your request of how it would be helpful for her to respond.

Failure

"I hate to fail, but I do. How does God view my failures?"

"Failure." Some of us don't allow the word into our vocabulary. Failure is what happens to others, or so we hope. But then it hits us again. How does God view our failures? First, they don't surprise Him. He knows we'll fail, and He loves us anyway. Isn't that great news?

"Failure" means to deceive or disappoint. *Webster's Dictionary* says failure is "the condition or fact of not achieving the desired end."[6] Is failure just the absence of success? Is it simply a matter of bombing out, of not completing what we set out to attain? Perhaps not. And failure isn't just the pain of a loss either. It's also the pain of a new beginning.

When we fail, we're tempted to blame someone or something, but let's leave God out of the blame loop. He *doesn't* cause our failures. He simply allows them to occur. Some failures involve sin, some don't. No matter what, God has promised to never leave us, forsake us, or turn His back on us. "The LORD is close to the brokenhearted and saves those who are crushed in spirit" (Psalm 34:18). "The LORD upholds all who fall and lifts up all who are bowed down" (145:14). Our

God is the God of second chances…and third and fourth and…

God wants us to know that in each failure lies a seed of potential growth. When you experience failure, do you judge yourself as having failed or do you judge that what you did failed? The difference is crucial. We can let failure cripple us or we can look to Scripture and see how God interacted with people who failed, including Noah, Abraham, Jacob, and Moses. He redeemed their shortcomings to accomplish His great purposes. Perhaps the best news of all is that God sees *beyond* our failure.[7] He's not stopped or hindered by our limitations. We may say, "Look how I've blown it, God. How can You ever love me again?" But God says, "Look how you've blown it. Let's discover what you can learn through this, and then I'll put the situation to use for the glory of my kingdom."

We tend to look at our lives through a microscope, but God looks at our lives with binoculars and says, "I see what you will accomplish for Me in the future. Take heart! I am with you." If that doesn't give you hope, nothing will!

What do you need to do to construct the way you see failure so it's based on God's view?

Faith and Integrity

"I'm no saint, but I want to take a stand for Jesus. How can I demonstrate my faith?"

This is a great goal! We need more men of integrity. "The one whose walk is blameless, who does what is righteous, who speaks the truth from their heart...will never be shaken" (Psalm 15:2,5). But integrity is a costly virtue. What are some of the costs? Time, effort, money, and perhaps even popularity and respect. Integrity isn't popular because it makes some people uncomfortable with their own ethics and decisions, especially in the business world.

"Integrity" means "sound, complete, without blemish, crack, or defect." In the construction business, integrity is created by adhering to building codes that ensure the building will be properly designed to be safe and function according to its purpose. Webster's dictionary has a simple word for integrity: "honesty."

"How will integrity make my life better? How will that draw people to Jesus?" you ask.

- Integrity helps you avoid problems. "The integrity of the upright guides them, but the unfaithful are destroyed by their duplicity" (Proverbs 11:3).

- Integrity gives you a solid footing. "The man of integrity walks securely, but he who takes crooked paths will be found out" (Proverbs 10:9).

- Integrity gives you something that lasts. "The days of the blameless are known to the LORD, and their inheritance will endure forever" (Psalm 37:18).

- Integrity provides a blessing for your children. "The righteous man leads a blameless life; blessed are his children after him" (Proverbs 20:7)…

- Integrity pleases God. "I know, my God, that you test the heart and are pleased with integrity" (1 Chronicles 29:17a).

- Integrity makes you more like Jesus. "'Teacher,' they said, 'we know you are a man of integrity and that you teach the way of God in accordance with the truth…'" (Matthew 22:16b).[8]

Embrace integrity. It's a hallmark of a righteous man.

Gift Giving

"I like giving and receiving gifts. What's one of the best gifts I can give my wife?"

A gift is selected with care and consideration to bring delight and fulfillment to another. Think of the care and effort you put into selecting a gift for the people you love. You feel excitement. There's challenge involved in selecting just the right item. A true "expression of love" is an act of grace—given whether the recipient deserves it or not.

Marriage is a gift! Your wife may be the finest gift you've ever received. You may be the finest gift your wife has ever received. As a gift to your partner, how do you live so that she feels blessed? Does she experience delight, fulfillment, and a feeling of being special when she's with you?

One husband's well-received gift to his wife was a special plaque:

> My gift to you is God's Word coming alive in my life. I will treat you and respond to you according to these passages.
>
> "Whatever is true, whatever is noble, whatever is right, whatever is pure, whatever is lovely,

whatever is admirable—if anything is excellent or praiseworthy—think about such things" (Philippians 4:8).

"Love bears up under anything and everything that comes, is ever ready to believe the best of every person, its hopes are fadeless under all circumstances, and it endures everything [without weakening]" (1 Corinthians 13:7 AMP, brackets in original).

Why not discuss these questions with your partner?

- What is the best tangible gift your partner has ever given you?
- What is the best tangible gift you've ever given your partner?
- What is the best intangible gift your partner has ever given you?
- What is the best intangible gift you've ever given to your partner?
- What gift would your partner most appreciate?

Identity

"My job gives me meaning and purpose. It's who I am. What happens if I lose my job or retire?"

It's true, creating our longstanding identities is a main struggle for people. Most of us base who we are on our performance and productivity. And since work today is unstable, a lot of men are suffering. Major transitions are taking place and will continue to do so as more companies focus on the bottom line instead of the workforce. Many of us in the prime of our lives are searching for available work of any sort. Some men have despaired and aren't bothering to look any longer.

Turning fifty today is an unavoidable risk because age and seniority are no longer a plus or part of a safety net at companies. When we've invested years in extra education or on-the-job training and the profession and/or company shrivels up, we may feel we have no place to go.

As men approach their forties, the former daydream questions of "How will I prepare for my next promotion?" and "What will I do with the added benefits?" change to nightmarish concerns: "How will I start over if I lose my job?" "How will I survive without work until I find new a new job…if I find a new job?"

Most people don't understand the desperate, deep despair not having a job creates within a man. At first we cope, but the coping is like a balloon blown up to cushion the blow. It says to others, "It's no big deal. I can handle it." Soon the balloon bursts. Take away our work, and we're in trouble. Our sense of purpose and the opportunity to do something constructive are woven into our thought processes and our perception of ourselves.[9] When we struggle with identity and ask, "*Who* am I?"—we're asking the wrong question. The right question is, "*Where* am I?" That question points to our identity in relation to God. Patrick Morley said, "We are who we are because of *where* we are."[10] Many hearing this take their task-oriented, male perspectives and ask, "Then what can I start doing for God?" Again, wrong question. It's not about *doing* things for God. It's simply *being* with Him.

If we're task-oriented in our relationship with God, we'll soon be asking, "What is the purpose of my life?" A more important question is, "*Who* is the purpose for my life?" That question focuses on a man's relationship with Jesus Christ. By answering the second question first, the first question is easier to answer.[11]

Can you answer "Who am I?" without talking about your career? Give it a try.

Loss

"I've had several major losses lately. I don't want to talk about it, but I'm struggling. When will it get easier?"

How do we usually respond to losses—big or small?

The Silent Treatment. Most men keep their feelings and thoughts bottled up. Men tend to *think* their way through circumstances. Thinking is done alone, so we seldom discover the details about what's troubling us because there is no explaining required. Questions aren't asked or answered, so no one helps us work through what we might miss on our own.

Most men tend not to share their problems with their friends. Women lighten the load by sharing the weight, whereas men get emotional hernias by carrying the load themselves.[12]

Going it alone. We often give excuses for what we're doing or why we're not at work rather than openly saying, "I was so overcome with grief over the loss that I wasn't able to function or help anyone. I was hurting." Sometimes we grieve alone to avoid burdening others. We grieve alone to avoid weeping in front of others. Some of us have never learned to cry outwardly, so we cry alone on the inside. When Scripture talks about Jesus weeping, it says simply, "Jesus wept." I think one of the most significant statements about tears was written by Max Lucado: "When words are most empty, tears are most apt."[13]

Taking Action. Another way men deal with loss is by taking action, which can be physical, such as a fight, or intangible, such as suing someone.

A Better Way

Sharing our feelings and losses with others is a better way to deal with pain and stress. "But how can we do that if we're wired and trained *not* to be this way?" you ask. Perhaps the answer is that a time of loss might be the opportune time to be different, to realize "I'm not in control of my life, and I don't have all the answers. I have an abundance of different feelings. My beliefs that *real men don't cry* and *it isn't safe to share* may not be accurate. There is a different, healthier way to live." Once such realizations take root, the door opens for growth and a healthier way of living.

Recommended Reading

H. Norman Wright. *Experiencing Grief.* Broadman & Holman, 2004.

H. Norman Wright. *When You Lose Someone You Love.* Regal Books, 2013.

Love Diminishing?

"Do I love my wife? Yep. But it's not as intense as it was. It comes and goes. The great feelings I used to have...well, I don't know. Love seems to have taken a nosedive."

"Diminishing love." Have you heard that expression? Maybe not, but you've more than likely heard the phrase "I fell out of love." How do you "fall out of" something like love? Before we go on, take a look at what you and your partner believe by answering these questions separately and then discussing them.

- My definition of love is...
- I believe my spouse's definition of love is...
- What are several reasons people give for falling out of love?

One of the leading counselors in the United States on this subject is Michele Weiner Davis. Consider her words:

> First of all, people don't just *fall* out of love. If love dwindles, it's because the marriage wasn't a priority. Love is a living thing. If you nurture it, it grows. If you neglect it, it dies.

What are those steps that you've taken this year to nurture your love for your wife? What does she do to demonstrate love to you?

The number one cause for the breakdown in marriages in our country is that people don't spend enough time together. They take their marriages and their spouses for granted. Keep track of the amount of quality time spent together—no kids or electronics.

Second, love isn't just a feeling, it's a decision. Happily married people understand that if they engage in activities that bring love into the marriage, they will *feel* loving. There is no magic or mystery here. What you decide to do on a daily basis will determine how much love you and your partner feel for each other.

To have a loving marriage, you have to put yourself out and love your partner the way he or she wants to be loved.[14]

Remember, the love that is needed to stabilize a marriage is the type of love God displays to each of us—unconditional commitment to an imperfect person.[15] How are you doing in that aspect?

Marriage Communication

"Scripture says, 'Husbands, love your wives, just as Christ loved the church' and 'husbands, love your wives and do not be harsh with them.' How do I do this?"

Here are "Ten Commandments for Loving Your Wife":

1. *Silence is not always golden,* especially between husband and wife. Ask your wife when she'd like to talk.

2. *When you love your wife, you take her feelings and viewpoints seriously.* When disagreement arises, say, "I see things differently, but you make good points." Believe it!

3. *Tell your wife how much you value her.* "A wife of noble character who can find? She is worth far more than rubies" (Proverbs 31:10).

4. *Don't stop at complimenting your wife once.* Look for something else nice to tell her.

5. *Instead of telling your wife what you don't like, tell her what you do.* For example: "I really like it when you try out new recipes on me."

6. *When your wife lets you know you've hurt or offended her, think about your goal to love before responding.*

Will you be defensive? Resentful? Humble? Sorrowful?

7. *Be your wife's companion.* When your wife is upset, exhausted, or overwhelmed, what she usually would like most of all is simple companionship. Be there for her. Your presence, patience, and prayers will help her feel loved.

8. *If you love someone you will be loyal no matter what the cost.* Always believe in her, always expect the best of her, and always stand your ground in defending her (see 1 Corinthians 13:7).

9. *Complaining about your wife won't improve your marriage.* Instead, tell her what you like about your marriage and make positive suggestions that include action on your part as well as hers.

10. *Don't suffocate your wife with possessiveness.* God is the one who owns us. He's merely entrusted your wife to your care. Ask her how she would like you to care for her in new and different ways, and then follow through.[16]

Midlife

"Is this a midlife crisis? My body doesn't cooperate at times, and I'm not as sharp as I once was. Is there a cure?"

Welcome to life's big transition. Some men dwell on their lives being half over; others focus on the half before them. Either way, hitting middle age can be a struggle.

Dissatisfaction can occur at any time, but it's especially common in middle age. Struggles with work, doubts about purpose, strains in the marriage, feelings torn when releasing children, parents needing help can dominate. Life may seem dull or profoundly routine. Some people aren't happy with where they are, where they've been, or where they think they're going.

For many, the sense of being discombobulated relates to identity and function. The roles people filled, the hats they wore, suddenly seem irrelevant or unimportant. Their identity is shaken as they wonder if what they do really matters.

The path to middle age usually has significant markers to guide us along the way, and these gave us security, a sense of direction, some predictability. Now some of the maps we've been accustomed to following are no longer there or are outdated.

Losses seem to increase, which can include vibrancy

and hope. Sometimes discouragement is a heavy weight. Paul Tripp said, "It's crushing to wake up to the fact that you long ago put away your satchel of dreams. It's hard to face the fact that you are more cynical than you are expectant."[17]

As we consider our bodies, we wonder if it's possible to be positive about aging. Some people feel dread as they experience heightened concerns about issues, such as weight, diet, and aches and pains.

In the form of general or specific regret, as well as dashed plans and unfulfilled dreams, disappointment can seep in. We can't seem to get motivated. We're missing our old spark...disinterest casts a dark shadow over us.

It's not uncommon to begin withdrawing to the point where distancing becomes a negative factor. We desire only to be left alone and feel irritated when people intrude.

If our adherence to long-held values begins to crumble, we feel increasingly distracted. There's so much occurring inside that's troubling so our resistance diminishes and temptations can seem overwhelming.[18]

So where are you now? Talk to God about how you're feeling and what you're experiencing. Read His Word for comfort and hope. Share what's going on with your wife and close friends. There is hope and strength in the love and fellowship of those around you.

Praying Together

"I'm a Christian so I pray, but I don't pray with my wife. People have told me it's really important. Why?"

Prayer is part of spiritual intimacy, and that is the foundation for emotional and sexual intimacy. Yes—sex.

The level of connection between you and God provides an important foundation for intimacy in your other relationships. Consider your own prayer life and relationship to Jesus Christ. As the level of communication deepens between you and God, you'll begin to experience greater strength and the courage to be more honest and open with your wife. God's plans for your marriage are best fulfilled when you are open to His presence and guidance. Prayer is really the first step toward marital intimacy.

The next step is sharing yourself with your wife by praying together. The majority of Christian couples don't exercise this privilege that can become such a special element in their relationships. Praying together will help you establish conversational intimacy too.

Unfortunately, many of us have never been taught how to pray as a couple. For most of us, developing an intimate prayer relationship with our spouse is an option we tackle with very little training or examples.

Getting Started

Praying together is a time of coming together in the presence of God. There is no "right" amount of time to spend praying. Often couples begin by taking a minute or two to share concerns and requests. Then they pray silently together. After establishing this practice they may feel comfortable praying aloud.

When you pray together communication barriers are broken, wills are made more pliable, and hearts reach out to each other. The honesty of praying together out loud to God in the presence of your partner allows you to be more open with your emotions and trust. And there is a safeguard that protects you as you open yourself to another person—God's love.

The Holy Spirit will minister to you and your spouse when, through prayer, you give Him access to your marriage. True intimacy begins between God and you and then expands to God and you and your spouse when you come before Him as a couple.

Romance—Part 1

"I've been married seventeen years. We used to be romantic, but that's diminished. I need some help."

A great way to rebuild this vital part of your relationship is to discuss the following questions.

Step 1

1. What is romantic about your daily life together? Be specific.

2. What actions on your part create romance for you? What actions on your spouse's part create romance for you?

3. Describe a romantic getaway you would like to experience with your spouse. Where would it be? What would you do?

4. What would it take for a romantic getaway to actually happen?

5. How could you create an "at home" romantic getaway?

Step 2

1. When we were dating, we created and sustained romance by...

2. When it comes to romance in our marriage now, my view is...

3. When it comes to romance...

4. Sometimes I get romantic, and you don't respond. When this happens, I feel...

5. Sometimes you get romantic, and I don't respond. When this happens, I feel...

6. Sometimes I'm unable to get romantic with you because...

7. One way I'd like us to be romantic at this point in our marriage is...[19]

Romance often includes the element of the unexpected. Presenting flowers or a gift for no special occasion or reason adds sparkle.

A second element in a romantic relationship is called dating.

Third, because romance is often emotional, sometimes the impractical adds a nice touch.

Fourth, don't be afraid to be creative.

Romance—Part 2

"I'm a romantic guy, but sometimes I'd really like to wow my partner. Any suggestions?"

I like what Joseph Dillow tells husbands about being creative lovers. He's developed the following test to help husbands evaluate their creativity in romance.

- Have you phoned her during the week and asked her out for one evening that weekend—without telling her where you are taking her? A mystery date.

- Have you given her an evening completely off? You clean up the kitchen; you put the kids to bed.

- Have you gone parking with her at some safe and secluded spot and kissed and talked for an evening?

- Have you drawn a bath for her after dinner? Put a scented candle in the bathroom, add bath oil to the bath, send her there right after dinner, and then you clean up and put the kids to bed while she relaxes. (My wife says in order to get any points for this you must also clean up the tub!)

- Have you phoned her from work to tell her you

were thinking nice thoughts about her? (You get *no* points for this one if you asked what was in the mail.)

- Have you written her a love letter and sent it special delivery? (First class mail will do.)

- Have you made a [recording] of all the reasons you have for loving her? Give it to her wrapped in a sheer negligee!

- Have you given her the day off? You clean the house, fix the meals, and take care of the kids. (My wife says you ought to get 30 points for this!)

- Have you spent a whole evening (more than two hours) sharing mutual goals and planning family objectives with her and the children?

- Have you ever planned a surprise weekend? You make the reservations and arrange for someone to keep the children for two days. Tell her to pack her suitcase, but don't tell her where you are going. (Just be sure it's *not* the Super Bowl!) Make it someplace romantic…[20]

Saying the Wrong Thing

"I guess I need some help with my mouth. I spout off and say the wrong things. Any help here?"

What are you using as a guide for what you say? You've got the best book available on what to say if you have a Bible. We all need to read it, digest it, and practice its principles. Let's take a look.

How many times are the words "tongue," "mouth," "lips," and "words" mentioned in the book of Proverbs?* The answer is coming later, but suffice it to say this book is the finest guide we can ever have on how to communicate. Consider the following guidelines on what *not* to say.

- Boasting: "Like clouds and wind without rain is one who boasts of gifts never given" (Proverbs 25:14). "Do not let any unwholesome talk come out of your mouths, but only what is helpful for building others up" (Ephesians 4:29).

- Flattery: "Whoever rebukes a person will in the end gain favor rather than one who has a flattering tongue" (Proverbs 28:23). Avoid using

---

* More than 150 times!

insincere compliments (deception) to get what you want.

- Verbosity: "Don't talk so much. You keep putting your foot in your mouth. Be sensible and turn off the flow!" (Proverbs 10:19 TLB). Don't fill the air with empty words.

- Argumentative: "An angry person stirs up conflict, and a hot-tempered person commits many sins" (Proverbs 29:22). Avoid rigidity, stubbornness, and unhealthy anger. Be purposeful, constructive, and helpful.

Here are some other passages in Proverbs on communication and anger for you to check out: 14:16-17; 15:4; 17:14; 17:22, 24-25. "Be kind and compassionate to one another, forgiving each other, just as in Christ God forgave you" (Ephesians 4:32). How do you see yourself living this verse out in a practical way? For example, how will you demonstrate kindness to your wife, children, and co-workers this week? Does this sound basic? It is—because this is where true communication begins.

Sex

"Yeah, sex is a big part of my marriage. Sometimes it gets routine. I hate to admit it, but I could use some help."

I encourage you to make your sexual experiences a marital priority and leap the hurdles to achieve that together. You and your partner need to create your own unique style to meet each other's sexual needs. "Love appointments" need not take the fun or spontaneity out of making love.

Sexual touching is a vital part of the husband–wife relationship. As with other forms of marital communication, touching takes time and effort to understand and continue to explore what works best for your partner and for you.

You will differ in your desire for expressing physical love. To increase the enjoyment of physical touching in your marriage, evaluate your present experiences. After each of you have completed the following statements separately, share your responses with each other.

- Some ways I like to be touched are…
- Some of the ways I don't like to be touched are…
- I think my partner likes to be touched…
- The times I like to be touched are…

Gary and Barbara Rosberg wrote, "Although sex can lead a couple into some of the most intense pleasure in a marriage, sex also has the potential to lead them into pain." Why is that true? First, because there can be misunderstandings between husband and wife. For example, men usually spell "intimacy" s-e-x and women usually spell "intimacy" t-a-l-k.

Second, most of us come to our marriages with unrealistic expectations built on media-promoted images of sculpted bodies and steamy seductions.

Third, our sexual lives can cause hurt because we too often see sexual pleasure as something we *get* rather than something we *give*. We're more focused on our own needs than on our spouses' needs. A great sex life leaves no room for selfishness.

Extremely satisfying sex occurs when husbands and wives connect the physical side with the spiritual, emotional, relational, and psychological sides of sex. When all these facets work together, couples enter the mystery of the oneness God intended. Great sex isn't just a grope, a grab, and a romp in the sack—although at times that can be satisfying. Great sex involves a lifetime of study, practice, commitment, discipline, and creativity.

Sex a Problem?

"Why are there so many conflicts around sex? Sex was God's idea, so why doesn't it work better?"

Let's look at some of the sexual differences between men and women.

- Most women give sex to achieve emotional closeness; however, men tend to view sex as being close.

- Women view sex as one way of being close, but many men view it as the only way to be close.

- Tenderness, touching, talking, and sex go together for a woman. Men think sex is sufficient for intimacy. It's easy for men to substitute sex for sharing.

Sex is an expression of emotion; however, for many men it serves as a substitute for emotion. One wife said:

> To me being close means sharing and talking. He thinks being close is having sex. Maybe that's the difference in the way we love. When he's upset or mad or insecure, he wants sex. I guess it reassures him. I wish he would talk about his feelings. When I get home from work and I'm wound up with a lot of baggage, I want to talk about it.

When he comes home that way, he doesn't want to talk. He wants sex.

One husband said:

Sure, sex means many things to me. Sometimes I want sex with my wife because I feel romantic and want to be loving and close. Other times I just want the release or diversion. I don't need to talk all the time about it. I wish she could understand that. It can't always be romantic.

Men tend to believe sex replaces other kinds of communication. We think sex suffices for sharing our personal and private selves. Husbands say to their wives, "You know I love you because I make love to you."

We also hesitate to discuss sex because we're afraid of making fools of ourselves. We're supposed to be the strong, tough, knowledgeable ones.[21] Men and women think every sexual experience should be a 10, and yet most of us have never read a book about sex. (I recommend *Sheet Music* by Kevin Leman, *The 5 Sex Needs of Men and Women* by Gary and Barbara Rosberg, and books by Cliff and Joyce Penner.)

Sex Questions

"I'm embarrassed because I've got a lot of questions about sex. Is that normal for guys?"

Yes, it is. Here are some survey results about sex. Why not step up and talk them over with friends?

- Men were concerned about being oversexed. Their questions were about expressing sexuality rather than the basics of arousal.

- A second question concerned being under-sexed.

- A third find on the survey was, "How can I control my sex drive?" [22]

What are men hesitant to bring up with women?

- Negative aspects of a spouse's physical appearance or character. Her weak points.

- Sexual fantasies. It may make the wife feel that she doesn't satisfy her husband.

- Less-than-satisfying sex. When I approach the subject I get negative responses.

- Seeing a beautiful woman gets my mind going. I don't think [my wife] would understand that I can be sexually attracted to other women.

Sex questions men asked in my counseling office:

- Can I be cured of sexual temptations?
- Is there help against pornography and fantasy?
- What do I do about sexual frustration?
- How can I control my desires and remain pure?
- How do I deal with obsessive sexual thoughts?
- Why did God give men such strong sex drives and women so little?
- What's the difference between intimacy and sexuality?
- How can I be close with someone and not be sexual?
- How do I deal with my fear of impotency?
- How do I handle sexual dysfunction?

So, what are your questions about sexuality? I recommend the books on this topic written by Cliff and Joyce Penner.

Sexual Fantasies

"I have sexual fantasies. I try to stop—but forget it. These come and go. Is this normal?"

You bet it is. The ability to think and imagine are gifts from God and part of being human. Fantasy is useful for building a good marital sex life. Unfortunately, it can also distort relationships if uncontrolled. But we shouldn't fear fantasy. Men and women use their imaginations to enhance many areas of their lives.

The apostle Peter wrote, "With minds that are alert and fully sober...do not conform to the evil desires you had when you lived in ignorance" (1 Peter 1:13-14). James stated, "Each one is tempted when he is drawn away by his own desires and enticed. Then, when desire has conceived, it gives birth to sin" (James 1:14-15 NKJV). Romans 12:2 talks about being "transformed by the renewing of your mind." Ephesians 4:23 NKJV says, "Be renewed in the spirit of your mind."

God ordained sex in marriage; therefore, sexual desire between mates isn't wrong.

We've been given the power to control our imaginations because imagination can eliminate thoughts that set healthy limits, distort wholesome sexuality, but also expand healthy fantasies. Sexual desire isn't wrong, but how we choose to use the desire can be.

The real problem is neglecting to control our eyes, our thoughts, and our impulses. Neglect of self-control of these senses can destroy relationships as well as reputations. Neither the look of recognition nor the look of admiration is an issue; however, the look of lust is a problem. Fantasy can distort reality. It hides blemishes, enhances curves, and blots out physical and personality flaws. No real person can compete with a fantasy. The more flawless and unreal the sexual fantasy, the less satisfaction there may be with a person's spouse.

So what can men do? We can use our sexual thoughts and responses in healthy ways. If you're a man, you're going to admire women. So admire. You're going to be sexually stimulated by what you see, so accept that reality but deal with it correctly. Don't feed it. Don't dwell on it. Turn your sexual responses toward your wife. Fantasize about her. Don't be afraid of your thought life. Bring your fantasies into your married sexual relationship.

If you'd like to overcome hesitation about discussing sexual issues with your wife and enrich your married sex life, read a book about sex out loud together. (You might start with the biblical book Song of Songs.) This may feel threatening at first, but the embarrassment can be overcome.

Sharing

"I wonder if I'm normal. There are a number of thoughts and subjects I hesitate to share with my wife. Is this typical?"

I asked men throughout the country, "What subject(s) do you think men hesitate most in bringing up or discussing with women?" These responses were submitted:

- "Anything personal." Particularly anything personal about themselves. I don't believe most men get into much self-examination. We feel it's tough to answer questions about how we feel, so sharing that would open the door to the dreaded follow-up question women tend to ask: "Why do you feel this way?"

- "Our insecurities, weaknesses, fears, vulnerability." So much of our identity (personally and culturally) centers on being strong and being "the protector." Sometimes we feel as though we can't show our vulnerabilities without compromising our masculine identity and role. That isn't true, of course. But knowing it's not so is a lot different than feeling it's not so.

- "Emotional intimacy." Sometimes it's hard for us to come up with the right words to say.

- Another subject that's difficult to discuss is the struggle with lust. The difficulty may be rooted in fear—fear of rejection, fear of hurting our wives, fear of facing our own corruption.

It's sad how much of our lives is dominated by fear. Ironically, we're being controlled by fear when what we really want is to be in control. Our emotional withdrawal costs us big time.

Excessive competitiveness and *personal dumping on ourselves* for underachievement are reflections of fear—of losing, failing, or being second best. We're afraid of being powerless and will go to extremes to be in control or avoid situations in which we might feel out of control. As a result, we're typically seen behind the wheel of a car rather than in the passenger seat—especially if our wives are with us.

We fear losing our manliness or having our sexual ability questioned, so we hide our needs and hurt by withdrawing and being silent. Thus, when we're encouraged to share our inner, personal worlds, those making the request may not understand the extent of the fears we're confronting and our hesitancy to be open.

Yes, my friend. You're a normal male.

Sharing How You Feel

"How do I get more comfortable sharing my feelings?"

First, never compare your skill level in sharing to a woman's ability. Unlike boys, girls learn to communicate emotions early. Don't let your wife's ability to communicate intimidate you. Your goal is to communicate your emotions in a way that's comfortable for you.

Second, realize that sharing your feelings brings a multitude of life-changing benefits. It helps you relate to God more. Psychologically and physically you'll be giving your wife one of her most desired gifts—true intimacy. And you'll be a great role model for your children.

Third, listen to how others describe their feelings. Make a list of feeling words and memorize them. Use these new words in sentences within your mind until you become comfortable with them.

Fourth, use "word pictures" to describe what's going on inside you. Instead of just saying, "I had a hard day," you can say, "Today was frustrating. At one point it felt like it was raining on everything I tried. I was really discouraged."

Fifth, try writing down what's going on inside you.

Sixth, if you usually say, "I think...," change it to "I feel" or "I felt" or "my inner reaction was."

Practice, pray, and know God will help you. And why not let your wife help?

1. Explain what you're doing and that it will be difficult. Let her know it would be helpful if she acknowledged your progress occasionally.

2. Let her know that sometimes the way you share may not seem clear and may differ from the way she'd share, and that's okay.

3. There will be times when you need to think through what you're feeling to access your emotions. Silence is okay.

4. Ask for understanding and grace. Tell her that when either of you share feelings, no judgments or criticisms should be given.

5. Ask for confidentiality when feelings are shared.

6. State clearly what you want. If you don't want to *discuss* your feelings but simply *state* them, let your wife know beforehand.

7. When your wife wants to discuss her feelings, make eye contact, listen carefully, and ask questions. Don't be defensive. Don't try to fix the problem for her.

Spiritual Apathy

"I read the Bible (some) and pray (sometimes), but my faith isn't growing. Any suggestions?"

It sounds like a "spiritual" eating disorder. You've heard of eating disorders—overeating, eating junk food, under-eating, anorexia, bulimia, and so forth. Usually we think of eating disorders being associated with women, but men engage in them too. A far more common "eating" disorder is spiritual. Anorexia is "body emaciation because of a physical aversion to food and eating." Bulimia is an "eat and then throw-up" disorder. Listen to how Steve Farrar describes these two disorders in the spiritual realm:

> Spiritual anorexia is an aversion to feeding from the Word of God. It is impossible for a man to stand and fight in spiritual warfare if he is spiritually malnourished. This is why the enemy will do whatever is necessary to keep us from reading and meditating on the Scriptures. Jesus put it this way in his dialogue with Satan: "Man shall not live by bread alone, but on every word that proceeds from the mouth of God."

If we're not consistently taking in the Scriptures,

then we will be weak and sickly and easily over-come by temptation. We may believe in the Bible and even revere it, but if we're not feeding from the Bible we are prey for the enemy. That's why the enemy attempts to disrupt the appointments that we make to meet with the Lord and His Word.

As dangerous as spiritual anorexia is, there is another disorder that is even more dangerous. Bulimia is an eating disorder that is commonly known as the binge-and-purge syndrome.

Spiritual bulimia is knowing the Word of God without *doing it*. Or as James described, it is *hearing* the Word of God without doing it…

Spiritual bulimia is characteristic of those who binge on truth: it can be through books, [record-ings], good Bible teaching, listening to a favorite communicator on the radio. That's why the spir-itual bulimic appears to be so righteous. There's just one problem. The bulimic knows the truth, but he doesn't apply it.[23]

When we're undernourished physically, the answer is to eat and digest food. When we're undernourished spiritually, the answer is to eat and digest more of the Word of God.

Strength

"I work out a lot because I want to be strong. Anything wrong with that?"

All of us like to be men of strength. It's part of being masculine. When you think of strength, what comes to mind first? Probably physical strength. We usually measure strength from a physical perspective. Pumping iron, running laps, doing curls, walking fifteen miles in three hours. We measure our ability in terms of endurance and strength. Physical fitness is big business these days. Just check out the sports club ads for examples of men of strength with great proportions. But to look like that takes time (and some of us never will no matter what we do).

There are other types of strength: strength of character, emotional strength, spiritual strength, to name several. Have you identified your personal strengths? Take the time to list them. Now, evaluate how they're being used. In what ways would you like to be stronger?

We're all weak in areas. If even the Man of Steel—Superman—has his kryptonite, is there any hope for us? There are many varieties of kryptonite out there. Some of it is attractive too. More money, a bigger house, a BMW, popularity with the guys, appreciative glances from attractive women. What are your weaknesses? When you encounter them, admit them, confess them to God, and ask Jesus Christ to help you. Do this often, and the kryptonite's hold weakens.

One last thought on strength. Do you want *real* strength? Spiritual strength that will see you through all difficulties? Well, there is a state of weakness that is more powerful than strength. It's when you acknowledge that you are insufficient and weak so you choose to lean on your Lord and Savior, Jesus Christ, who suffered and died for you. Through Him real strength comes. He is your trainer who will get you into condition.

Go to your Master—Jesus Christ. Invest your time with Him and His Word. You'll discover and acquire more strength than you thought possible! "[Jesus said,] 'My grace is sufficient for you, for my power is made perfect in weakness.'" The apostle Paul said, "I will boast all the more gladly about my weaknesses, so that Christ's power may rest on me. That is why, for Christ's sake, I delight in weaknesses, in insults, in hardships, in persecutions, in difficulties. For when I am weak, then I am strong" (2 Corinthians 12:9-10).

Stress

"I've got a lot of stress in my life. Sometimes I think I feed on it. It keeps me going. Is that okay?"

"Good stress" involves a brief feeling of exhilaration. Bad stress brings about long-term psychological and physical erosion. So much of the stress I see in people who seek counseling has to do with feeling out of control. Getting fired, having a child injured, suffering when a spouse is disabled, and dealing with a parent's sudden stroke are all examples of things we can't control.

There are four factors that will help you distinguish between good and bad stress.

Sense of choice. If you *choose* something that carries a sense of pressure, it often feels more like stimulating motivation instead of stress.

Actual control. Those who have a need for control experience greater stress when they aren't in control. Feeling out of control can involve very simple situations:

- We're stressed when we are forced to be in the passenger seat rather than at the wheel of an automobile.

- We're stressed when we have to wait for a table at

a restaurant, or in line for a movie, and frequently choose to forgo the meal or movie to regain our sense of choice.

- We become infuriated by road construction and exasperated at "stupid" drivers who distract or detain us...

- We postpone dental appointments and other procedures that require us to put ourselves in another's hands.

- We prefer requests to demands, and free choice to requests—and we demonstrate this by saying "no" to suggestions for things that we might actually have enjoyed.[24]

Ability to anticipate consequences. It's more difficult for some to make the necessary adjustments when consequences—expected and unexpected—occur.

Attitude. How we view and approach issues contributes to how stress affects us. We have more stability and less stress when we rely on a biblical perspective.

You choose your response to life's difficulties. How can these verses help you decrease daily stress? "Consider it pure joy, my brothers and sisters, whenever you face trials of many kinds, because you know that the testing of your faith produces perseverance" (James 1:2-3).

Time

"The older I get, the more I seem to slow down. How do I continue to make a difference?"

We all want to make a difference. What we're really asking is, "What does God want to accomplish through me during this season of life?"

Jesus said, "Love the Lord your God with all your heart and with all your soul and with all your mind...[and] Love your neighbor as yourself" (Matthew 22:37, 39).

So many people have told me that what made the difference in their lives was knowing they were loved. Who knows you love them? How do they know? Saying "I love you" makes a huge difference!

My brother and I have been close all our lives. We know we love each other, but we never said it. Quite a few years ago I was a hospital in Los Angeles while my wife Joyce underwent brain surgery. I was talking to my brother on my cell. At the end of the conversation, he signed off with "I love you," and I responded in like manner.

As I walked back inside the waiting room, I wept. What an overwhelming gift to hear "I love you" from my brother. Ever since then, we've ended each conversation that way. Why didn't we share those words before? I have no idea. But I'm glad we do it now.

We should never assume another person knows we love them. Ken Gire addressed this concept:

> So it's the end of the day, and each of us is lying in our bed, reflecting. Have I loved well? Has love been the beating heart pushing through all my conversations? Seen in my eyes? Felt when other people are in my presence? Was the truth I spoke today spoken in love? Were the decisions I made today based on love? Were my reactions? My devotions?
>
> Have I loved well?
>
> If we can answer yes to that question, it is enough.
>
> It may not be enough for our employer...[for] our fellow workers...[for] all the carpools and committees and other things on our calendar.
>
> It may not be enough for us.
>
> But it is enough for God.
>
> And that should make it enough for us.[25]

We need to ask ourselves, "Did I love and live well today?" And if the answer is no, we need to figure out what to do differently tomorrow.

Notes

1. Paul Tourneir, MD, *Learn to Grow Old* (London: SCM, 1971), 192.

2. Patrick Morley, *The Man in the Mirror* (Grand Rapids, MI: Zondervan, 1997), 58-59.

3. Gary B. Rosberg, *The Sex Needs of Men and Women* (Wheaton, IL: Tyndale, 2006), 19-21, adapted.

4. Michael McGill, *The McGill Report on Male Intimacy* (San Francisco: HarperCollins, 1985), 269, adapted.

5. Ken Druck, PhD, with James C. Simmons, *Secrets Men Keep* (New York: Doubleday, Inc., 1985), 35-36, adapted.

6. *Webster's New Riverside University Dictionary,* 2nd ed. (Boston: Houghton Mifflin, 1984), s.v. "failure."

7. Gary Oliver, *How to Get It Right When You've Gotten It Wrong* (Wheaton, IL: Victor, 1995), 66-78, adapted.

8. John Trent and Rick Hicks, *Seeking Solid Ground* (Colorado Springs: Focus on the Family, 1995), 58-60, adapted.

9. John Munder Ross, *The Male Paradox* (New York: Simon & Schuster, 1992), 179, 183, adapted.

10. Patrick Morley, *The Seven Seasons of a Man's Life* (Nashville: Thomas Nelson, 1995), 58-59, adapted.

11. Ibid., 145.

12. McGill, *McGill Report,* 176, adapted.

13. Max Lucado, *No Wonder They Call Him the Savior* (Portland, OR: Multnomah Press, 1986), 106.

14. Michele Weiner Davis, *The Divorce Remedy* (New York: Simon & Schuster, 2001), 54-55.

15. Ibid., 95-96.

16. H. Norman Wright, *How to Really Love Your Wife* (Ann Arbor, MI: Servant, 1995), adapted.

17. Paul Tripp, *Lost in the Middle: Midlife and the Grace of God* (Wapwallopen, PA: Shepherd Press, 2004), 39.

18. Ibid., 38-41, adapted.

19. David Luecke, *The Relationship Manual* (Columbia, MD: The Relationship Institute, 1981), 74, adapted.

20. Joseph Dillow, *Solomon on Sex* (Nashville: Thomas Nelson Publishers, 1977).

21. McGill, *McGill Report*, 58, 188-189, adapted.

22. Ibid.

23. Steve Farrar, in Bill McCartney, et al., *What Makes a Man* (Colorado Springs: NavPress, 1992), 58-59.

24. R. Kent Hughes, *Disciplines of Grace* (Wheaton, IL: Crossway Books, 1993), 187.

25. Ken Gire, *The Reflective Life: Becoming More Spiritually Sensitive to the Everyday Moments of Life* (Colorado Springs: Chariot Victor, 1998), 85-86.